The Language Experience Approach for Teaching Reading

A Research Perspective

Second Edition
1978

Reading Information Series:
Where Do We Go?

by MaryAnne Hall
Georgia State University

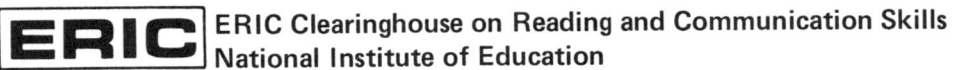
ERIC Clearinghouse on Reading and Communication Skills
National Institute of Education

International Reading Association
800 Barksdale Road, Newark, Delaware 19711

IRA PUBLICATIONS COMMITTEE 1977-1978 *Chairing,* Harold L. Herber, Syracuse University • Janet R. Binkley, IRA • Faye R. Branca, IRA • Roger Farr, Indiana University • Mary S. Feely, IRA • Lynette Saine Gaines, University of South Alabama • Margaret Keyser Hill, Southern Illinois University • Laura S. Johnson, Morton Grove, Illinois • Lloyd W. Kline, IRA • Connie Mackey, Montreal, Quebec • John McInness, Ontario Institute for Studies in Education, Toronto • John E. Merritt, Open University • Theodore A. Mork, Western Washington State College • Clifford D. Pennock, University of British Columbia • Emma W. Rembert, Florida International University • Robert B. Ruddell, University of California at Berkeley • Cyrus F. Smith, Jr., University of Wisconsin at Milwaukee • Zelda Smith, Gables Academies, Miami • Ralph C. Staiger, IRA • Carl Wallen, Arizona State University • Sam Weintraub, State University of New York at Buffalo.

ERIC/RCS Staff Editor: Kathryn Grossberg

Published December 1977

ERIC Clearinghouse on Reading and Communication Skills
1111 Kenyon Road, Urbana, Illinois 61801

International Reading Association
800 Barksdale Road, Newark, Delaware 19711

Printed in the United States of America

The material in this publication was prepared pursuant to a contract with the National Institute of Education, U. S. Department of Health, Education and Welfare. Contractors undertaking such projects under government sponsorship are encouraged to express freely their judgment in professional and technical matters. Prior to publication, the manuscript was submitted to the International Reading Association for critical review and determination of professional competence. This publication has met such standards. Points of view or opinions, however, do not necessarily represent the official view or opinions of either the International Reading Association or the National Institute of Education.

The International Reading Association attempts, through its publications, to provide a forum for a wide spectrum of opinion on reading. This policy permits divergent viewpoints without assuming the endorsement of the Association.

Library of Congress Cataloging in Publication Data

Hall, MaryAnne.
   The language experience approach for teaching reading.

   (Reading information series)
   Published in 1972 under title: The language experience approach for the culturally disadvantaged.
     1. Socially handicapped children—Education—Reading. 2. Socially handicapped children—Education—Language arts. I. Title II. Series
LC4086.H3 1978   371.9'67   77-26983
ISBN 0-87207-861-2

Foreword

ERIC/RCS and IRA are concerned with developing several types of information analysis and disseminating this data to audiences with specific professional needs. It is primarily the producer of research—the research specialist, the college professor, the doctoral student—to whom the Reading Information Series: Where Do We Go? has been addressed. ERIC/RCS is pleased to respond to the expressed needs of reading educators by cosponsoring with IRA the second edition of MaryAnne Hall's *Language Experience Approach for Teaching Reading: A Research Perspective.*

The language experience approach is the focus of both Hall's 1972 edition, titled *The Language Experience Approach for the Culturally Disadvantaged* and originated by ERIC/CRIER at Indiana University, and the present one; however, in the second edition, the coverage is broader. One reason for this is that the application of language experience learning and teaching for special populations encompasses much that is appropriate for *all* learners. Furthermore, this edition includes much research on the language experience approach that does not concentrate primarily on lower socioeconomic levels, material that would have been excluded by a narrower scope.

The focus of this book rests clearly on the *extension* of research and development activities: "Where do we go?" The intent is not to provide an exhaustive review of the literature. Rather, it is to present the thoughtful recommendations of a researcher whose experience and expertise have led her to a firm and well-considered position on the language experience approach.

The purpose of this and other books in the series is to strengthen future research in reading education. The Reading Information Series contributes helpful perspectives on the research literature and suggestions to those who perform research in reading and related fields.

Bernard O'Donnell
Director, ERIC/RCS

Introduction

Interest in, and application of, the language experience approach to the teaching of reading and other communication processes have expanded markedly since the late 1950s. As attention to the approach has increased, so has the amount of research investigating the achievement of students instructed with this approach. Not only have researchers investigated achievement in this approach, but they have also begun to examine particular dimensions of the approach, such as oral language growth, the nature of the content of children's productions, and affective factors.

The following definition is the one intended throughout this volume. The language experience approach for teaching reading is a method in which instruction is built upon the use of reading materials created by writing down children's spoken language. The student-created reading materials represent both the experiences and the language patterns of the learner. The communication processes of listening, speaking, reading, and writing are integrated in language arts and reading instruction. While *language experience approach* (LEA) is the most common name for instruction of this description, other terms, such as the *language arts approach* (LAA) or an *integrated language arts program* are often used.

The preceding definition was used as one criterion for choosing research reports for this review. In some studies of programs called language experience, the feature of materials created by children was missing. Such studies are not included here. Some studies were of such short duration that they were excluded, unless the focus was on a particular learning process or element instead of on achievement. Some studies, in which the language experience component was combined with other programs in such a way that it was not possible to study its effect, were also omitted.

The purpose, then, of this volume is to examine the available research literature through a narrative review followed by a synthesis of research findings. Recommendations for future research constitute the final section of the report. It is not the intent of this review to discuss methodology. For the reader who wishes such information, the extensive discussions in a number of other sources are recommended (Allen 1976; Ashton-Warner 1963; Hall 1976; Lee and Allen 1963; R. Stauffer 1970).

Review of Literature

This review of language experience research is arranged, for the most part, with consideration to chronological order. Some grouping of studies is according to topic or level or some other characteristics of the population studied. Other published reviews of language experience research are cited first, followed by discussion of specific studies. The National First Grade Studies, including several follow-up studies, by the U. S. Office of Education constitute the last section of this literature review.

Research Reviews

Before 1970, with the exception of the literature review section in doctoral dissertations, few reviews of research in the language experience approach were available. In the earliest review located, Wrightstone (1951) concluded that language experience material can be used with effective results. Wrightstone had concluded in an earlier article (1944) that, by the end of the third grade, typical children taught systematically by activity-related (usually experience-oriented) methods were reading as well as were children taught exclusively with basals, when reading achievement was measured by standardized tests.

The second review of research and literature, by Hildreth (1965), provides an excellent historical perspective of the evolution of the language experience approach, from its classroom origins around 1900 through the studies investigating the approach from 1926 to 1965. The term *experience method* did not appear until 1934, and *language experience* was introduced still later. The name "language experience approach" did not signify the same instructional program from classroom to classroom or from study to study, and this variation in program still exists today.

Of the thirteen studies Hildreth cited, three had children of low socioeconomic level as the subjects. It is interesting to note that Hildreth does discuss the rationale for using the language experience approach with children of backgrounds different from the content common in commercial materials for reading instruction. She repeats the information reported in the Wrightstone review and adds studies made after 1951. She concludes that, by the end of third grade, typical children taught systematically by experience methods combined with individualized reading were reading as well as, or better than, children taught with basals. Two of the thirteen studies reported negative results from the language experience approach. However, one of those compared an incidental approach with systematic instruction, whereas the other studies examined carefully planned and executed teaching of reading within a language experience framework.

It should be remembered that the early research was limited in scope, and close scrutiny shows that the studies failed to meet many criteria of control. However, the Hildreth review is an excellent source for those wanting information about the early research on the language experience approach.

The third review of language experience reading instruction appeared in the 1967 conference proceedings of the International Reading Association (Vilscek 1968). This analytical report concentrated on the language experience projects in the National First Grade Studies.

Chall (1967) conducted an intensive analysis of research on beginning reading from 1910 to 1965, comparing code-emphasis approaches and meaning-emphasis approaches. The studies she reported do not relate directly to the language experience approach, although she does describe language experience, in a chapter on approaches. Chall's thoroughness is impressive, but the omission of language experience studies indicates a lack of attention to the approach, both in instructional programs and research programs.

A general review of the language experience approach made by Madison (1971) includes discussion of related books, articles, and materials sources; it mentions three of the first grade studies which were continued through the third grade.

Instructional procedures constitute the focus of a research review by Russell Stauffer (1976): he compiled summaries of eighteen studies "concerned primarily with comprehension as achieved by means of global language-experience procedures" (p. 1). In addition to reports of the individual studies, there are an introduction and an insightful position paper by Stauffer. Since the review follows a global definition of language experience learning that includes directed reading/thinking procedures, some of the studies cited in Stauffer's collection are omitted here, although many cited by him are discussed. There is no other source that presents summaries of selected language experience studies as clearly as *Action Research in L.E.A. Instructional Procedures* (R. Stauffer 1976).

Narrative Review of Selected Research

The specific studies reported in these reviews were examined, and certain of them will be discussed, along with other pertinent research. Studies included here are those which, for the most part, were (1) focused primarily on the language experience approach, (2) of sufficient duration to evaluate the factors studied, and (3) based on a definition of the language experience approach that is similar to the definition previously stated. Some studies were excluded because they used a "language experience reader" or other materials which were not created by students, and others were excluded because the language experience component was not investigated as a distinct variable. However, research which may not have had the language experience approach as a major focus is cited occasionally to illustrate a direction that future research may take or to document a lack of attention to this approach.

One of the early studies (Meriam 1933) advocated using the language experience approach with Mexican-American children whose background made existing books inappropriate. (In fact, the language experience approach is being mentioned currently as an approach for Spanish-speaking children whose language and cultural background are different from the language of the school and of commercial reading materials.) Meriam's research (1933) was a two-year study of eighty primary-grade children in a school which placed the instructional emphasis on such activities as construction, handwork, story telling, free reading, and dramatization for functional teaching of reading when needed in conjunction with the activities. Meriam concluded, "In general, the data indicate a highly satisfactory achievement of these pupils." Progress was reported in terms of months of progress on reading tests in comparison with months in school, but there was no control group for comparison. Considering that two-thirds of the children had IQ scores below 100, the gains stated are impressive.

In England, Gardner (1942) compared an experience-activity, or informal, approach with a formal approach, for a three-year period, for children of ages five to eight. She reported no significant differences in achievement in reading, spelling, or punctuation, at the end of the three-year period. Factors less directly related to the academic instruction, such as attitudes, imaginative painting, concentration, and social behavior, favored the experimental children. Gardner reported also that there was a slight tendency in the lower socioeconomic levels for the experimental pupils to do more poorly than the controls, but detailed analysis by socioeconomic level was not a major concern of the study.

In one large-scale investigation, three approaches to the teaching of reading, individualized reading, basal readers, and the language experience approach were studied during the 1959-1960 school year under the Reading Study Project conducted by twelve elementary school districts in San Diego County, California. Sixty-seven teachers participated. This project was the first large-scale one to employ the language experience approach, and the general conclusion was that the language experience approach, during the first three years of elementary school, can be an effective way of teaching reading. The language experience teachers found that children made as much, or more, progress in the reading skills, measured by standardized reading tests, as did children who were taught the skills directly (Allen 1962; San Diego Board of Education 1961).

Hall (1965) developed and evaluated a language experience approach for culturally disadvantaged Negro children in the Washington, D. C., schools for the first semester of the first grade.* There were 151

---

*The term *culturally disadvantaged* appears occasionally in this review, when it is the designation used by a researcher to describe the population or focus of a particular study.

pupils in the five experimental classes and 125 pupils in the five control classes. Significant differences between the groups, favoring the experimental group, were reported in gains made on measures of reading readiness, in word recognition on a standardized reading test, and in sentence reading on a standardized reading test. No significant difference was found in word recognition scores on a test of preprimer and primer vocabulary, developed by the investigator. Of the two approaches, teachers rated the language experience approach significantly more effective than the basal approach, though they indicated no differences in the practicality of the two approaches.

A culturally disadvantaged population was also used in Lamb's (1971) investigation of the effectiveness of the language experience approach for beginning reading with children in five first-grade classes in Indianapolis. The achievement and attitudes of the experimental group were compared to the achievement and attitudes of five control classes which used a modified basal reader approach. No significant differences in achievement and attitude were found using the *California Reading Test* and *The Primary Pupil Reading Attitude Inventory.*

Several studies were conducted at the University of Idaho to investigate the effects of a Communication Skills Through Authorship Program (CSTA). The CSTA program was considered supplementary; it consisted of having students dictate stories on a cassette tape recorder and then recite transcripts of their dictation. Schomer (1972) studied the reading achievement of first-grade and second-grade children using the CSTA program and reported that CSTA was "effective" in primary reading at the end of first grade and second grade. G. Harris (1972) reported that the reading achievement scores on the Stanford Reading Test for students in first, second, and third grade were significantly higher for those involved in the CSTA program.

Willardson (1972) reported that, in second grade, CSTA children's performance was higher on all measures of writing maturity than was the performance of children not in the experimental program. Significantly higher scores were reported for average sentence length and for average number of embeddings. In Owens' (1972) study of the CSTA program, the writing of third-grade students was investigated. Teachers rated the CSTA students more creative than the non-CSTA students, but the analysis of creative stories showed no significant difference in creativity rating between stories written by CSTA pupils and those by children not involved in the CSTA program.

Oehlkers (1971) studied the contribution of creative writing performance to the reading achievement of four first-grade classes that used the language experience approach. Two experimental classes began creative writing early in the year, while the two control classes did not begin creative writing until the second semester. Oehlkers found no significant difference in word recognition scores and concludes that students who receive early training in creative writing achieve as much word-recognition skill as do those who concentrate principally on reading activities during the first half of first grade.

While data on spelling is included in a number of studies, only one study was concerned primarily with spelling. In his doctoral dissertation, Cramer (1968) investigated the spelling ability of first-grade classes that received language arts reading instruction and the ability of classes that received basal reading instruction. He concluded that the language arts classes spelled regular and irregular words with nearly equal proficiency, whereas the basal classes spelled regular words with somewhat greater facility than they did irregular words. The language arts classes spelled both regular and irregular words significantly better than the basal groups, when performance on phonological spelling lists was compared. The language arts classes spelled words in written composition with significantly greater accuracy than did the basal reader classes.

Reading readiness is a concern of several language experience studies. Brazziel and Terrell (1962) conducted a study in which a six-week readiness program for one class of twenty-six culturally disadvantaged children emphasized the use of experience charts. These researchers found that experience materials provided meaningful reading content for disadvantaged children when used in connection with other readiness activities and materials. Since this program was a combined one, the effect of the experience materials alone is not known, but the scores on the Metropolitan Readiness Test administered at the end of the study were significantly higher for the experimental group than for three control classes.

O'Donnell and Raymond (1972) compared a conceptual-language readiness program and a basal-reader workbook approach to readiness, using kindergarten children in Maine. While the conceptual-language program may not be strictly a language experience program with heavy stress on materials created by children, emphasis on basic language understanding, such as "reading is enjoyable," were featured. After 116 days of instruction, analysis of readiness scores showed that the conceptual-language classes received statistically higher achievement scores and scored significantly higher on a measure of visual discrimination, but there was no significant difference between experimental and control classes on the Wepman Auditory Discrimination Test. O'Donnell and Raymond also reported no observable change in children's adjustment in either program. They reported that, at all intelligence levels, there were significant gains favoring the experimental group, and the most pronounced difference in favor of the language-centered program was for the low-ability group.

Reichbach (1973) compared two types of readiness programs, an informal language epxerience program and DISTAR, with kindergarten children. Three classes of lower socioeconomic level students were in each treatment group; subjects totaled 122. The posttesting showed that the DISTAR children scored significantly higher in two of the four subtests, and their total scores on the Wide Range Achievement Test also were significantly higher.

Weber (1975) studied readiness by comparing language experience and phonics readiness programs of six-weeks duration for postkindergarten children. Parents administered the programs with guidance from educators. At the conclusion of the program, significant differences in favor of the language experience group were found on readiness tests given at the beginning of the first grade. Reading achievement was tested at the end of first grade, but a number of first-grade variables, in addition to the pre-first-grade readiness program, may have affected reading achievement.

Another topic investigated in language experience studies is oral language. Giles (1966) compared the oral language development of four first-grade classes, two instructed with the language experience techniques and two using basals. He concluded that the language experience children made greater gains in oral language than did pupils instructed with basals and that the language experience advantage was greater for boys than for girls in developing oral vocabulary.

Cox (1971) studied samples of spontaneous expression, dictation, and personal authorship by twenty-five first-grade students in Tucson, Arizona, using the Cox Language Analysis Scale. As a result of her analysis, she reported that the language skills used in the three productive language situations studied were interrelated.

The purpose of Christensen's (1972) study of kindergarten children in Delaware was to study the effects, after five months, of two instructional programs, one with a language experience component and the other without, on freely produced oral syntax. She concluded that teaching approach, social class status, and sex did not exert a significant effect on the oral language facility of kindergarten children, as measured by changes in T-unit length, although there was a significant difference, favoring the language experience group, in the number of T-units produced. She did conclude that, for middle-class boys and girls, changes in syntactic development are likely to be greater in a language experience program, while the changes in syntactic development of lower-class children are likely to be similar in either program.

Analysis of the content—particularly of vocabulary—of language experience materials is featured in some research. Packer (1970) analyzed the vocabulary used in the experience materials of disadvantaged children in Philadelphia; Jacksonville, Florida; Jonesboro, Arkansas; and Yakima, Washington. He compared the "key vocabulary," words children said they wanted to know, with the vocabulary in the preprimers and primers of four basal series. In one of the school systems, there was a positive correlation between the key vocabulary and the basal vocabulary, but Packer concluded that there is a significant difference between the vocabulary which is meaningful to culturally disadvantaged children and the vocabulary contained in basal readers.

Another comparison of the vocabulary of disadvantaged children and the vocabulary of basals was reported by Cohen and Kornfield (1970). They found little divergence between selected basal reader lists and the oral vocabulary of black, lower socioeconomic level kindergarten students. They maintained that a meager vocabulary cannot be blamed for lack of reading achievement by low socioeconomic level students.

A case study analysis of students' written and taped responses provided the data in Stockler's (1971) research. The topical content of children's dictation and composition was investigated for black, culturally different, inner-city fifth-grade and eleventh-grade children with reading disabilities. Stockler reported that, for both age levels studied, "self" was the overwhelming concern, with family, friends, school, recreation and the black image as frequently recurring themes. It was concluded that students who had experienced severe reading failure could be motivated with language experience materials expressing concerns about themselves, their culture, and their lives.

Both Baxley (1972) and Dzama (1972, 1975) have analyzed the relationship between language experience vocabulary and word-attack generalizations. The topic of Baxley's dissertation was the utility of the forty-five generalizations studied by Clymer, when applied to the oral vocabularies of economically limited, Spanish-surname children. He found that seventeen of the eighteen generalizations identified by Clymer were useful with language experience vocabulary, but he also reported that seven other generalizations met the criterion of utility. Baxley concluded that, in language experience reading programs, there would be numerous examples for teaching word-attack generalizations. Dzama analyzed the vocabulary acquired (in word banks) by first-grade children using a language experience reading program. She found that the eighteen phonic generalizations that Clymer reported to be useful, as well as two additional ones, were illustrated sufficiently in the examples in the language experience vocabulary. Like Baxley, Dzama concluded that adequate examples for word-analysis study were present in a language experience program.

Henderson, Estes, and Stonecash (1972) studied the size and the nature of the reading vocabulary of 594 pupils in twenty-one first-grade classrooms in Prince George's County, Maryland, using a language experience reading approach. An anaylsis of the words accumulated in the word banks of twenty-five subjects showed that half the words were in the first thousand on the Lorge-Thorndike list. These researchers concluded that the vocabulary learned by midyear in a language experience program compares favorably with the extent of the vocabulary learned in a basal approach.

The acquisition of a reading vocabulary has been a concern of a number of researchers. Shears (1970) conducted an experiment using auditory and visual methods of teaching word recognition to American Indian kindergarten children. He used words from first-grade basals and words used by children in everyday life. While he reported no difference according to method, he did report that more of the words actually used by children were learned and retained than were the basal words.

Bennett (1971) compared the retention by four-year-old and five-year-old subjects on word-learning tasks involving words requested by the individual child, words mentioned by Ashton-Warner as those her students had requested, and words from Scott, Foresman basal readers. This study found that memory of the words selected by students was better than was memory of words from the other two categories. Bennett concluded that emotionality and meaningfulness account for the superiority of word learning based on self-selection.

McC. Gallager (1975) also studied vocabulary retention. She compared the thirty lower-class students instructed by language experience with thirty lower-class students instructed with a basal approach. This short-term study involved the teaching of three lessons in a one-week period, the experimental group receiving language experience treatment while the control group received basal instruction. The students were pretested, they were tested immediately after instruction, and they were tested after three weeks. No significant differences in vocabulary retention were found between treatment groups; however, the language experience group used a vocabulary that was more extensive than the basal's controlled vocabulary. Because the language topic was chosen for the children in the experimental group, the validity of the approach used as language experience can be questioned.

Kelly (1975) compared the performance of a group of third-grade corrective and remedial readers who had been instructed with a language experience approach with the performance of a group of third-grade remedial readers who had been instructed with a basal approach. She reported that, after fifteen weeks of instruction, the experience group had a basic sight vocabulary that was twenty-two percent greater than the vocabulary of the basal group. She also reported that the mean word-recognition score was the same for both groups but that sixty-two percent of the experience group exceeded the mean, while only thirty-six percent of the basal group exceeded the mean.

Duquette (1970) investigated the effect of a supplemental "key vocabulary" program on the reading and writing achievement of first-grade and second-grade children. His analysis of scores on the Stanford Achievement Test showed that experimental first-grade children scored better than children in the control group did on measures of word reading, paragraph meaning, and word-study skills, and the writing-sample analysis showed that their writing was significantly better in terms of the number of running words, words spelled correctly, different words, and polysyllabic words. Duquette reported that the experimental second-grade group did better than the control group did (but not significantly so) in terms of the number of running words, words spelled correctly, and different words. Only in the number of polysyllabic words did the control pupils exceed the experimental pupils.

The standard versus nonstandard language issue was reflected in Cachie's (1973) study. She hypothesized that kindergarten nonstandard-dialect speakers instructed by means of a language experience approach requiring a verbatim recording of their ideas would perform significantly better in reading comprehension, visual discrimination, and word knowledge than would those instructed by means of a language experience approach in which the dictation was recorded in standard English. The subjects were only nonstandard-dialect speakers without any previous reading training: each treatment group consisted of thirty students. After two months of instruction, no significant differences between groups were found when students were tested for reading comprehension on the Gray Oral Reading Test and for visual discrimination and word knowledge on the researcher's tests. The limited time period may have been one reason for the no-difference finding.

Divergent dialect was also the topic of Cagney's (1977) study. She investigated the listening comprehension of forty-eight black-dialect-speaking kindergarten and first-grade children when language experience stories were presented in their dialect and in standard English. First-grade children made significantly more correct responses than did kindergarten children. For both age levels there were significantly more correct responses to comprehension questions when stories were presented orally in standard English than when the stories were presented in black dialect.

Twenty fourth-grade remedial students participated in Wells's (1975) study to determine the feasibility of using wordless picture books and nonnarrated films as stimuli to produce language experience materials to facilitate reading achievement. Oral and written language samples were analyzed by T-units, with a one-group, pretest/posttest design. He reported that growth in reading vocabulary, comprehension, and total reading scores was significant above the .05 level. Growth in oral language facility, including total words, T-units, and words per T-unit, was above the .05 level, although there was no significant increase in words per T-unit used in written language. There was no statistically significant difference in students' reading attitudes.

Affective factors have been the major focus in some studies. The purpose of Knight's (1971) study was to determine differences in attitude toward reading after one school-year of instruction in four different beginning reading programs. Language experience, a bilingual program, the Miami Linguistic Readers, and basal readers were the methods used. Two second-grade classes and two first-grade classes from each of four schools were used in the study. The mean attitude scores on an attitude scale developed by the investigator were higher for second graders than for first graders, and significant differences in attitude favored the bilingual and Miami Linguistic Readers approaches.

Riendeau (1973) investigated the effects of language experience and basal reader instruction on the concepts of self-esteem, social interest, individuation, complexity, realism, and identification with mother, father, teacher, and friend. The subjects were 124 first-grade students divided equally between an experimental group using a language experience approach and a control group using basal readers. At the end of first grade, the language experience group "was found to have developed significantly greater self-esteem, social interest, individuation, realism, identification with friends, and preference for friends" than did the basal group. Features of this study were the detailed investigation of a number of affective factors and the stress on the affective climate desirable in language experience classrooms.

Mendenhall (1973) investigated the effect of a supplemental language experience program on the self-acceptance of second graders. The subjects were Chicano students in Colorado who were involved in programs of writing and reading stories about themselves, developed through self-acceptance activities. No significant effect on self-acceptance was found for students in the language experience program.

Barnette (1970) analyzed the effect of a supplemental key vocabulary program on attitudes toward reading and toward self. Her subjects were first-grade and second-grade students in Arizona. Attitude toward self was evaluated by analyzing students' drawings of themselves, and a twenty-six-item pictorial differential scale was used to determine positive or negative attitude toward reading. Barnette reported that first-grade pupils in the key vocabulary program developed significantly more positive attitudes toward themselves and toward reading than did a control group, but no significant differences were reported for second graders.

In comparison to the number of studies at the elementary level—especially studies of beginning reading—the number conducted with students above elementary level is limited. R. Stauffer and Cramer (1967) reported a cooperative venture between the State of Delaware Vocational Education Department and the Reading Study Center of the University of Delaware. This language arts program was designed to improve basic communication skills. Spelling and writing were correlated with experience stories. Directed reading/thinking activities used with the Rochester Occupational Series were also a part of the language program. There was no evaluation of reading skills, although the authors reported that the progress was "often dramatic" when these job-training enrollees were given the opportunity to read and write about matters of high personal interest. The in-service training was considered a primary objective of the program. While formal evaluation is lacking, the program does provide an example of language experience activity that could be used with adults.

Becker (1970) reported a program used in the Women's Job Training Program in Charleston, West Virginia, with four illiterates who ranged in age from sixteen to eighteen. The experience accounts used for instruction had a vocational orientation. At the beginning of the program, these four subjects were classified as nonreaders, but, after eleven months, their scores on the Spache Diagnostic Reading Scales were 2.8, 3.3, 3.8, and 5.5. Although these scores reflect the lower limits of the standardized test and are not instructional levels, Becker reported that, at the end of the project, two students were being instructed on a third-grade level; one on a fourth-grade level; and one, on a fifth.

Wilson and Parkey (1970) reported a program in a middle school in Charles County, Maryland, in which one low section of thirty-one rural, disadvantaged, and educationally retarded seventh graders was instructed with language experience procedures, by three teachers, in social studies, science, and mathematics. Three criteria were used in pretreatment/posttreatment comparison: (1) student self-evaluation, (2) teacher evaluation, and (3) student performance on a test of reading. A control group of seventh graders slightly less retarded than the students in the experimental group was used for the comparison. After the program, students in the experimental group appeared to view themselves more favorably as learners, while they rated themselves as readers about the same as they had before the program. Little difference was evident in the reading gains of either group on the only measure of reading achievement, the Botel Word Opposites Test. Teachers' ratings of the students at the end of the study were more favorable for the experimental group than for the control group, and, in fact, ratings of the control group were less favorable than they had been at the beginning of the study. The researchers reported a favorable reaction of the teachers to the accompanying in-service training.

Calvert's (1973) study was one of the few to concentrate on language experience programs for the secondary level: he developed a teaching guide for language experience activities. Seventh-grade and tenth-grade remedial Mexican-American students were the subjects in his study, although the classes that received language experience instruction included Anglo students. Vocabulary, comprehension, writing, attitudes toward teachers, use of reference materials, and use of graphic materials were evaluated. Calvert reported significant differences in pretest and posttest mean scores on attainment of originality and interest in writing samples by seventh-grade and tenth-grade students; significant differences between pretest and posttest mean scores of vocabulary in grade seven; significant differences between pretests and posttests of comprehension, use of reference materials, and use of graphic materials in both grades seven and ten; and significant differences in grade seven in pretest and posttest attitudes toward teachers. He concluded that a language experience program at the secondary level can be helpful in teaching reading and writing.

Mallett (1975) investigated the efficacy of the language experience approach with twenty-one North American Indian remedial junior high school students in British Columbia, Canada. Gains were measured in vocabulary, comprehension, writing achievement, and attitude. The students using the language experience approach were compared with students using a traditional reading-laboratory approach after eight weeks of instruction, and a second comparison was made after another eight weeks during which the groups switched approaches. Some of the experimental subjects received the language experience treatment first; some received that treatment second. No statistically significant differences were reported on measures of vocabulary and comprehension, although significant differences in gain, in favor of the experimental group, were reported for both writing and attitude.

Two studies used language experience materials while investigating the cloze procedure. The intent of the Kingston and Weaver (1970) research was to study the predictive value of the cloze test. A cloze task presented to first-grade rural disadvantaged students was based on material taken from language experience stories. Balyeat and Norman (1975) also investigated the use of the cloze procedure with language experience materials to test the comprehension of students. Language experience materials were collected from grades one through nine, and selections judged to be representative of each grade level were used to prepare testing materials. These were used in thirteen Appalachian counties, one year with children in grades two and five, and the next year with children in grades three and six. For these cloze selections, lexical items were deleted instead of every fifth word, the standard deletion form. LEA-cloze scores were correlated with selected subtests of the Stanford Achievement Test. The researchers reported "moderate to strong positive correlation between the LEA-cloze and the SAT." They suggest that the LEA-cloze procedure can be valuable in either predicting or indicating reading levels.

Efforts to document the extent to which the language experience approach actually is used is evident in some research. In one of the best-known surveys of reading programs of school systems throughout the United States, Austin and Morrison (1963) reported that only one school system out of the sixty-five surveyed employed the language experience approach as the major approach to beginning reading, although, in eighteen school systems, experience charts were used in conjunction with basal readers.

Hoover (1971) traced the historical development of the language experience approach and conducted a questionnaire survey of selected teacher-education institutions in the United States, to determine the extent to which teachers and future teachers are exposed to a language experience approach. She concluded that, prior to 1960, only limited exposure to a language experience program was evident in teacher education programs. However, she also concluded that, in the decade of the 1960s, professors increased both their knowledge of, and receptiveness to, the language experience approach.

Carstensen (1972) investigated the extent to which the language base of Allen's three-strand description of the language experience rationale is provided for in teachers' guides to the first-grade reading textbooks adopted in Arizona. Her investigation of five pages from each of seventy-seven examples revealed little emphasis on the use of dictated stories for writing and reading.

Questionnaire responses were used as the source of data in Staton's (1974) effort to obtain information about the extent of use of the language experience approach in beginning reading in forty-four open schools in three midprairie states. She reported that teachers and principals indicated they were eclectic in their approach to beginning reading and that language experience was included as an instructional approach for beginning reading.

A 1975 publication of the National Right to Read Effort and ERIC/RCS, *Effective Reading Programs*, which describes 222 reading programs, summarizes a number of programs that rely totally or in part on the language experience approach. While language experience programs are not in the majority, they are well represented.

The First Grade Studies

A major research investigation in the 1960s, the First Grade Studies were sponsored by the U. S. Office of Education to compare the effectiveness of various approaches in teaching beginning reading. Of the twenty-seven separate projects, six investigated language experience approaches (Hahn 1966; Harris and Serwer 1966; Kendrick 1966; McCanne 1966; R. Stauffer 1966; Vilscek, Morgan and Cleland 1966). Another study (Horn 1966) concentrated on language differences and readiness for culturally different, Spanish-speaking children. Of the six studies that dealt with language experience approaches, one (Harris and Serwer 1966) dealt specifically with the disadvantaged. The language experience studies were continued through the second grade, and some were reported through the third grade (Harris and Morrison 1969; Stauffer and Hammond 1969; Hahn 1968; Vilscek and Cleland 1968).

Hahn (1966) directed the Oakland, Michigan, project that examined the relative effectiveness of three approaches: (1) modified language experience with traditional orthography, (2) modified language experience with the Initial Teaching Alphabet (i.t.a.), and (3) basal readers. Results at the end of the first year showed no one method to be consistently superior to the other two. The students in the language experience approaches achieved significantly better scores on word reading and on spelling. Analysis of data obtained by matching the children according to socioeconomic backgrounds "failed to add much useful information."

The CRAFT Project—Comparing Approaches in First-Grade Teaching with Disadvantaged Children—(Harris and Serwer 1966) was designed to compare the skills-centered approach with the language experience approach for teaching beginning reading to disadvantaged urban children. Four methods were examined: (1) the skills-centered approach adhering closely to instruction manuals; (2) the skills-centered approach using the phonovisual method instead of the word-attack lessons in basals; (3) the language experience approach; and (4) the language experience approach with heavy audiovisual supplementation.

The basal approach produced a slight, but not significant, lead in achievement at the end of the first grade. The language experience approach with audiovisual supplementation matched the skills-centered approach in results and achieved better results than did the language experience approach alone. The investigators concluded that most culturally disadvantaged children can make substantial progress in learning how to read, even if their readiness scores are poor, and that culturally disadvantaged children can be taught to read with the same methods that work with advantaged children.

Kendrick (1966) compared the effectiveness of the experience approach with that of the traditional basal approach by analyzing children's performance according to socioeconomic level: high, middle, and low. He reported that, for most of the analyses performed, there were no significant differences between the experience approach and the traditional method. The language experience approach did affect favorably the interest of the lower-class males, however, and resulted in significant differences in the number of words in the writing samples of both boys and girls.

McCanne (1966) investigated three methods of teaching Spanish-speaking children in Colorado: (1) the conventional approach to English readiness and basal readers; (2) a modified approach to teaching reading as a second language (TESL); and (3) the language experience approach. He found that the basal reading approach developed the highest achievement in reading skills. McCanne suggested that the cultural patterns of these children may not encourage free participation in such group activities as discussion and that teachers may have been unfamiliar and uncomfortable with approaches (1) and (2). He did observe that nothing in his study was unfavorable toward the use of the TESL and language experience approaches for developing oral English skills and for enriching experience.

R. Stauffer (1966) compared a language arts approach to beginning reading with a basal reader approach, studying 433 students in twenty first-grade classes in Delaware. The language arts approach resulted in significantly higher scores on word reading, paragraph meaning, and spelling, but no significant differences were found in word study skills, vocabulary, or attitude. Pupils taught by the language arts approach did significantly better in writing mechanics, spelling, and number of words used in writing and scored higher on oral reading accuracy (but not on rate). A group of segregated Negro children was included in the experimental group, and these children's scores were lower than the rest of the experimental population; however, they had scored lower in reading readiness and intelligence at the beginning of the study, as well.

The Pittsburgh project (Vilscek, Morgan, and Cleland 1966) compared the achievement of children from three socioeconomic levels in a coordinated basal language arts program with those in an integrated-experience communication program. The experience group scored significantly higher on word meaning, paragraph meaning, vocabulary and word study, attitude, and creative writing. The higher socioeconomic level children scored higher in reading than did those on the middle level, and the middle level children scored higher than did those on the lower socioeconomic level. The basal approach resulted in higher achievement by lower socioeconomic boys than did the language experience approach, but the higher achievement of the boys in the basal group can be attributed to their higher reading-readiness scores.

Horn (1966) focused on reading, for a group of culturally disadvantaged, Spanish-speaking first-grade children. Three methods were used: (1) audiolingual techniques in English, using science-based materials; (2) audiolingual techniques in Spanish, using science-based materials; and (3) readiness techniques recommended by the San Antonio school district. The stress in the twenty-eight first-grade classes was on developing language and experience background. There were no significant differences in the mean reading scores of the different treatment groups. Horn claims there is a great need for new, more suitable measures of readiness, intelligence, and language competence for Spanish-speaking children.

Five of these first-grade projects studying the language experience approach were continued through the second grade. Four of the projects have been followed through the third grade.

Hahn (1967) reported that, at the end of the second and third grades, the language experience pupils, using either traditional orthography and i.t.a., scored better on reading and spelling tests than did the children instructed with basals. The differences between language experience pupils using i.t.a. and those using traditional orthography were very slight.

The CRAFT project extension (Harris, Serwer, and Gold 1967) at the end of the second grade included 666 children. At this time, the basal reader group had the highest scores in word knowledge and spelling, although the differences between groups were not statistically significant. Great range was reported within the methods but not between them. The children who participated in the project scored better than did comparable second-grade children in the same schools who did not participate in the project.

Vilscek (Vilscek, Cleland, and Bilka 1967) reported that the language experience pupils scored higher on spelling tests and attitude measures but that there were no significant differences on tests of word meaning, word-study skills, and language skills. After the third year, Vilscek and Cleland (1968) reported no significant differences between methods, although they did report relationships between achievement and socioeconomic level and mental age.

Kendrick and Bennett (1967) reported that, at the end of second grade, twelve of the comparisons made in their study favored the language experience group and eleven favored the traditional group. They found that boys of lower socioeconomic level did better with the language experience approach.

The third-grade extension of the CRAFT project in New York City (Harris and Morrison 1969) and the Delaware study (Stauffer and Hammond 1969) do not significantly alter the earlier conclusions. The CRAFT third-year report again stated that the means *within* methods differed more than the means *between* methods. In the first and second grades, the mean score for the skills-centered approach was slightly higher, and, in the third year, the language experience group scored slightly higher in achievement, but not significantly so.

In Delaware, the third-year language experience classes scored significantly higher on spelling, on accuracy and rate of oral reading, on word recognition, on measures of creative writing, such as writing mechanics, spelling, number of running words and different words used, and on number of polysyllabic words. The conclusion reached was that an eclectic language experience approach will yield good results in reading throughout the primary years.

In summarizing the language experience and basal comparisons in the Cooperative Research Projects, Bond and Dykstra (1967b) explained that relatively few significant differences were found between the approaches. The significant differences that did exist generally favored the language experience approach. However, the authors caution that these "sporadic differences were not of much practical significance in terms of actual reading achievement" (p. 120). Their analysis of the studies led Bond and Dykstra to these conclusions: (1) The success of the language experience approach indicates that the addition of this approach to a reading program can be expected to make a positive contribution to that program. (2) A writing component is likely to be an effective addition to a primary reading program.

R. Stauffer and others (1972) extended the original Delaware first-grade project through the sixth grade. Of the initial total of 576 subjects, 334 remained through the sixth year. Results favoring the experimental (language arts) approach were reported for word knowledge, reading, written language usage, and creative thinking; yet the researchers report that the findings "are suggestive rather than definitive." The researchers did present evidence that an eclectic language experience program can be successful, but they were concerned about the many features of inquiry and other scholarly attributes that were featured in the instruction but were not tested.

Another spin-off of the Delaware project was the analysis by R. Stauffer and Pikulski (1974) of the oral language reflected in the notebook of stories dictated by fifty children in first-grade classrooms using the language experience approach. A comparison was made of dictation taken in the fall of the first-grade year and dictation taken in the spring. Significant improvement was noted in all evaluated dimensions of oral language (average number of words, average number of sentences, average number of long sentences, average number of short sentences, average number of pronouns, average number of prepositions, average number of different prepositions, average number of different words). The researchers commented on the verification this study provides of the substantial linguistic growth of children involved in language experience instruction.

M. Stauffer (1973) followed the original Delaware project in the First Grade Studies, using the same schools and the same basic research design. Her purpose was to investigate the comparative effects of a language arts approach (LAA) and a basal reader approach (BRA) on the reading achievement of first-grade pupils tested at the end of first grade and at the beginning of second grade. The teachers' knowledge of innovative procedures, the use of additional testing programs, and extended analyses of data were the major variables altered from the first study. The sample of 564 pupils included ten LAA classes and eleven BRA classes. According to Stauffer, "in view of the results of this study, one can tentatively conclude that first grade children taught to read in a LAA program as prescribed in this study by teachers knowledgeable of the teaching procedures will achieve better in reading and creative writing than pupils taught to read by teachers with years of experience with basal reader manuals."

Scores obtained on all measures of reading achievement except rate of oral reading showed a significant difference in favor of the LAA groups. All LAA groups except the groups with IQ below 70 scored significantly higher than the BRA groups; there were no significant differences in the groups below the 70 IQ level. The LAA groups in the study scored significantly higher on reading subtests of the Scholastic Aptitude Test than did the LAA groups of the earlier study by R. Stauffer and Hammond. There were no significant differences between the first and second studies in the scores of the BRA groups.

Synthesis

The research does substantiate that the language experience approach is an effective way to teach reading and related communication skills. The following synthesis of that research is organized topically, with discussion of general achievement, readiness, oral language, vocabulary, word analysis, creative writing, spelling, comprehension, use with special populations, affective factors, teacher education, and language differences.

Comments on the limitations of some studies and the extent of coverage are included in the final part of this section.

Achievement

Studies investigating the effectiveness of an instructional approach usually measure achievement in reading. Since a considerable amount of the language experience approach has been of the method-comparison type, achievement is reported in a number of the language experience investigations. The often-quoted conclusions of the National First Grade Studies, (Bond and Dykstra 1967; Dykstra 1968) that no one method was consistently superior and that there was more difference within methods than between methods, seem appropriate in regard to reading achievement in language experience programs.

There is research evidence to support that the overall reading achievement of students who receive language experience instruction is satisfactory, and, in some cases, it is superior to the achievement of children instructed by other approaches. The early studies cited by Hildreth (1965), the three-year study in San Diego (Allen 1961; San Diego Department of Education 1961), two of the Communication Skills through Authorship project studies (Schomer 1972; G. Harris 1972), and the language experience projects in the National First Grade Studies (Hahn, A. Harris, Kendrick, McCanne, R. Stauffer, Vilscek, and others) along with the M. Stauffer replication, were the major studies to emphasize reading achievement, although reading achievement was investigated in a number of other studies reported in the literature review section.

Research comparing one method with another is not as prevalent in educational research as it was from 1920 to 1965. In recent years, language experience research has been less likely than before to be a methods-comparison study; it is more likely to be an investigation of a specific question, focusing on concerns other than general achievement.

Readiness

The language experience approach is more widely used at the beginning reading stage than at any other level of reading development. Yet, while generally acknowledged as an excellent means of introducing children to reading, reseach on language experience programs for prereading instruction is relatively limited.

Brazziel and Terrell (1962) reported that the use of experience charts in a readiness program provided meaningful content for children of low socioeconomic background; the experimental group using charts obtained higher readiness scores on the Metropolitan Readiness Test than did the control groups that did not use the experience materials.

Hall (1965) concluded that the language experience approach was superior to the basal approach for encouraging the reading readiness of inner-city pupils, when, after a semester of instruction in first grade, gains on the Metropolitan Readiness Test were analyzed.

Horn (1966) was concerned with the effectiveness of three methods of developing reading readiness in Spanish-speaking children. Although the methods he studied were not specifically language experience ones, he stated that new readiness programs are needed that stress language development, extension of experiences, and favorable self-concepts.

Bond and Dykstra (1967a) state there is some indication that low-readiness pupils perform better in a basal program, whereas high-readiness pupils are more successful with a language experience program. However, they suggested that sampling problems may have contributed to the appearance of this tendency.

O'Donnell and Raymond (1972) reported that children in a conceptual-language readiness program scored significantly higher gains in readiness than did children who used a basal readiness workbook. They reported that, while the readiness gains were significant for all ability levels, the most pronounced difference in favor of the language experience approach was for the low-ability group. The experimental group scored significantly higher in visual discrimination and higher, but not significantly so, on letter names, but no difference was reported for the Wepman Auditory Discrimination Test.

Weber (1975) reported that children who participated in a language experience readiness program conducted by parents performed significantly better on a readiness test than did children who had been given phonics instruction by parents.

While oral language was the major consideration in Christensen's (1972) study, the language experience program was developed for readiness.

Except for these studies, language experience readiness programs generally have not been studied. The study of readiness in language experience programs reflects concern with test results and demonstrates little regard for specifics in terms of the nature of the programs or the characteristics of the students. Although discussions of readiness in reading-methods textbooks and in instructional programs usually focus on a number of factors in children's backgrounds (cognitive, physical, perceptual, linguistic, environmental, and so on), as well as on specific instructional areas (visual and auditory discrimination, left-to-right orientation, letter-name knowledge, for example), prereading language experience research, for the most part, is devoid of such specificity.

Oral Language

The significance of oral language in language experience programs is immense. Language experience programs stress the integration of all language arts, and oral communication is the base for written language products in language experience instruction. The oral language factor, however, has received little attention in language experience research.

Although it is limited, the research on oral language use and development in language experience programs shows generally favorable results. On this topic of oral language development, careful description of the actual instructional program is particularly essential, in order to evaluate the research results.

Giles (1966) reported that first-grade pupils using the language experience approach made greater gains in oral language than did pupils using a basal approach.

Cox's (1971) analysis of samples of spontaneous expression, dictation, and personal authorship showed that the language skills used in the three activities are interrelated.

Wells's (1975) research with remedial students showed significant growth in oral language facility when oral language samples were measured by gains in total number of words, number of T-units, and number of words per T-unit.

Christensen (1972) reported no significant differences in effect on children's oral language facility, in terms of mean T-unit length, between a language experience kindergarten program and a regular kindergarten program. She did report that, for middle-class children of both sexes, changes in syntactic development are likely to be greater in a language experience program, but the changes are likely to be similar in either program for lower-class children. R. Stauffer and Pikulski's (1974) analysis of the oral language reflected in the stories dictated by first graders revealed significant improvement in all evaluated dimensions of oral language.

Vocabulary

Vocabulary in language experience research can be analyzed according to the nature of the words used and learned by children, as well as according to the extent of the vocabulary learned.

The emotional impact on children of the vocabulary they use in language experience activities has been of interest ever since the appearance of the "key vocabulary" concept associated with Sylvia Ashton-

Warner's (1963) teaching of Maori children in New Zealand. Bennett (1971) reported that children four and five years old more readily remembered words they requested than they did other words (from Scott, Foresman basals and words reported by Ashton-Warner as frequently requested). Bennett concluded that emotionality and meaningfulness account for the superior recall of one's own words. Shears (1970) also reported that American Indian kindergarten children retained more words they actually used than words from basals.

Packer's (1970) analysis of the vocabulary identified by children and of the vocabulary in preprimers and primers showed a significant difference between vocabulary that is meaningful to culturally disadvantaged children and the vocabulary used in basals. However, Cohen and Kornfield (1970) found little divergence between the vocabulary in basal readers and the oral vocabulary of black, urban kindergarten children of low socioeconomic level. They concluded that lack of conceptual vocabulary cannot be used as an excuse for reading retardation in the primary grades.

Documentation of vocabulary learning in the language experience approach can be found in several studies. Henderson, Estes, and Stonecash (1972) reported that the vocabulary of first graders, after four months of instruction by the language experience approach, compared favorably with the vocabulary learning of children instructed with basals. Kelly (1975) reported that a group of third-grade remedial students using language experience had a basic sight vocabulary that exceeded the vocabulary of a basal group after fifteen weeks of instruction.

Hall (1965) reported a statistically significant difference in achievement in favor of the language experience group, on the vocabulary (word recognition) portion of a standardized test. On a measure of preprimer and primer vocabulary, no significant difference was found between the language experience and basal groups.

McC. Gallager (1975) reported no significant difference in vocabulary retention between students who received three language experience lessons in one week and students who received a comparable amount of basal instruction, when vocabulary learning was tested three weeks after instruction. She did report more extensive vocabulary use of the language experience students. The nature of the program as language experience in this instance is questionable, since the topic was selected by the investigator: thus the meaningfulness factor may not have been significant.

A persistent criticism of language experience instruction is that students may not develop a satisfactory reading vocabulary, since the lack of vocabulary control and the lack of systematic repetition may be detrimental to learning. The research refutes this criticism. Language experience instruction presents learners with meaningful vocabulary, and a reading vocabulary *is* acquired by learners through the use of LEA.

Word Analysis

There is some concern that word anaylsis instruction may be slighted in language experience programs. Baxley and Dzama studied the extent to which the vocabulary used in language experience programs provided examples of common phonic generalizations. Baxley (1972) concluded that children's oral vocabulary provided ample examples for teaching phonic generalizations. Dzama's (1972, 1975) examination of the reading vocabulary in the word banks of language experience students in first grade showed that language experience material furnishes children with adequate examples for learning selected orthographical regularities.

Because of the confusion of the terms *word recognition* and *word analysis*, it is difficult to separate reports of children's ability to use mediated word-recognition strategies from reports of vocabulary knowledge, which is often what may be measured by tests labeled "word recognition."

Creative Writing

Creative writing should flourish with the language experience approach, since the approach is based on children's expression of original ideas, first through dictation and then through independent writing. Measures of writing performance and of creativity have been incorporated in a number of language experience studies. The research on writing performance in language experience programs is particularly impressive.

In the second year of the Delaware project, Stauffer and Hammond (1967) reported that an analysis of creative-writing performance indicated the language arts group wrote significantly longer stories, used a significantly more-varied vocabulary, spelled significantly more words correctly, and performed significantly better in terms of writing mechanics than did the basal reader group. These results suggest strongly that the language arts approach develops a greater facility in written communication than does the basal approach.

Measures of writing were also taken in the other First Grade Studies language experience projects and, where reported, also favored the language experience groups. Bond and Dykstra (1967b) reported that a writing component added to a regular reading program enhances achievement in reading. This finding was noted in both the i.t.a. projects and the language experience projects, and it is supported by the work of Kendrick (1966), McCanne (1966), and Vilscek, Morgan, and Cleland (1966).

Oehlkers (1971) reported that the early emphasis on creative writing in first grade enhanced achievement in word recognition as much as did early emphasis on reading activities.

One project, Communication Skills through Authorship (CSTA), in Idaho, placed considerable emphasis on creative writing. The dissertations of Willardson (1972) and Owens (1972) considered creative writing by primary students. Willardson reported that second-grade students scored higher on all indices of writing maturity than did children who did not participate in the CSTA program. However, only two measures, average sentence length and average number of embeddings, showed a significant difference. Owens (1972) studied the effect of CSTA on the writing of third-grade students. Outside judges rated creative stories by CSTA students and by children who had not participated in the CSTA program. The analysis revealed no significant difference in creativity between the experimental and control subjects. Teachers' observations that CSTA children were more creative were not substantiated by the story analyses.

Wells (1975) reported growth in written language facility for fourth-grade remedial students. He found that there was a significant difference in the total number of words and T-units used but reported no significant increase in words per T-unit in written language.

M. Stauffer (1973) compared two groups of first graders: the experimental group used a language arts approach to reading, and the control group used a basal-reader approach. On a measure of creative writing, a random sample of the experimental group scored significantly higher on diversity of vocabulary, story content, mechanics of writing, and spelling.

Spelling

Spelling performance of children in language experience programs has been reported in some research, though only Cramer (1968, 1970) has made spelling the sole concern of a language experience investigation. He reported that first-grade language experience students spelled both irregular and regular words significantly better than did students taught by a basal approach. In addition to better performance on tests of spelling ability, the language experience students spelled significantly better in written composition than did the basal students.

R. Stauffer (1966) reported that the language arts pupils in his project of the First Grade Studies spelled significantly better than did children instructed with basals. This finding was confirmed in the second and third years of the study. M. Stauffer (1973) reported better spelling performance for language experience students at the end of the first grade. In another First Grade Studies project, Hahn (1966) reported no significant differences between the spelling performance of students instructed by i.t.a., the language experience approach, or basal readers, when spelling in i.t.a. was accepted for the i.t.a. group. At the end of the second year, Hahn (1967) reported better spelling performance for language experience and i.t.a. students than for basal students.

The researchers who have investigated spelling achievement usually comment on the spelling progress fostered by the opportunities to write that are offered in language experience programs. One reason spelling has not been examined more closely in language experience research may be that many of the studies are conducted with beginning readers, and intensive work in spelling usually comes after some reading base has been acquired.

Comprehension

When the reading achievement of children receiving language experience instruction has been tested, comprehension may be measured, although the actual test may be titled "paragraph meaning," "sentence meaning," or simply "comprehension." The work of Balyeat and Norman (1975) provides one example of using the cloze procedure with language experience materials to test comprehension.

Specific questions about comprehension in language experience programs seem not yet to have been asked for research purposes. The rationale statements for the language experience approach put great stress on reading as communication and on the concept that language experience material is meaningful for the learner; thus, from the beginning of reading instruction, the learner should view reading as comprehending written language. On the other hand, a frequently stated criticism of the language experience approach is its failure to encourage students to learn to understand ideas written by those other than themselves and their peers.

The Use of the Language Experience Approach with Special Populations

Attention to language experience programs for special populations is evident throughout language experience research, from the early studies to the present. The special populations identified here are linguistically different children, students from lower socioeconomic levels, remedial students, and adult illiterates.

Merriam (1933) used the language experience activity approach with Mexican-American students and reported impressive gains in reading achievement. Calvert's (1973) research concluded that a language experience program can enhance the writing achievement of Mexican-American students, as well as their reading-study skills. Mendenhall's (1973) investigation of self-acceptance in a language experience program was conducted with second-grade Chicano children.

North American Indians in British Columbia were the subjects in Mallett's (1975) research. He reported that, though the junior high school students instructed by the language experience method showed no significant differences in reading vocabulary and comprehension gains compared with students instructed with basals, there were statistically significant differences, in favor of the language experience group, in writing gains and attitude gains. Shears (1970) also used a Native American population in his study of vocabulary learning.

The effectiveness of language experience programs for children from low socioecnomic levels was demonstrated by Hall (1965) and by the CRAFT project (A. Harris and Morrison 1969; A. Harris and Serwer 1966; and A. Harris, Serwer, and Gold 1967). Harris and Serwer (1967) maintained that most children from lower economic levels can make substantial progress in learning to read in spite of low readiness scores and that they can be taught to read by the same methods that work for middle-class children.

While there seems to be considerable discussion about the applicability of the language experience approach for special populations, in articles, speeches, and books about language experience programs, there have been few major research efforts to study the language experience approach for special populations, except for the National First Grade Studies projects with populations from low socioeconomic levels.

Wells (1975) concluded that the language epxerience approach is an effective means of developing remedial fourth-grade students' reading abilities, oral language, and written language abilities. Wilson and Parkey (1970) reported favorable results were obtained by using a language experience program in the content areas for remedial seventh-grade students. Calvert (1973) concluded that, for remedial secondary students, a language experience program can enhance writing achievement, reading, and study skills.

Stockler (1971) concluded that "students who had experienced severe reading problems could be motivated by stimuli to write and illustrate stories, poems, and essays and read their own materials." She commented on the eloquent descriptions produced by fifth-grade and eleventh-grade black inner-city students about their lives.

Becker (1970) and Stauffer and Cramer (1967) have investigated the language experience approach to reading for adult illiterates. No recent research relating to the use of the language experience approach with adults was located.

Affective Factors

Proponents of the language experience approach stress the affective factors that contribute favorably to learning, and researchers have studied the attitudes, toward reading and toward themselves, of children who have been instructed by the language experience approach.

A. Harris (1969) reported striking differences between the skills-centered approach and the language experience approach in the results of positive and negative motivation. At the first-grade level in language experience classes, positive motivation tended to go with good achievement and negative motivation with poor achievement. In the second grade, positive motivation was associated with good achievement in the language experience classes and with poor achievement in the skills-centered classes. Negative motivation was associated with poor achievement in both basal and language experience classes.

Wilson and Parkey (1970) reported improvement in middle-school students' view of themselves as learners after receiving language experience instruction. No significant differences on measures of the self-acceptance of second graders were found by Mendenhall (1973) in her investigation comparing language experience with other methods. Becker (1970) noted improved attitudes and self-concept in illiterate Job Corps trainees after language experience instruction. Another report of significant gains in attitude for students in a language experience program is Mallett's (1975) study.

M. Stauffer (1973) reported no significant differences in attitude toward reading, as measured on the San Diego Reading Attitude Inventory, between a first-grade group instructed by a language arts approach (LAA) and a basal-instructed group, but the LAA group showed a significantly better attitude toward reading when this was measured by the number of books reported as having been read during a specified monthly period.

Riendeau (1973) reported that first-grade children instructed by a language experience approach developed significantly greater self-esteem, social interest, individuality, identification with friends, and preference for friends than did children instructed by a basal approach. The specificity of factors studied in this investigation contrast with the common practice of studying a general "attitude," "self-concept," or "acceptance" factor. Reindeau stressed the significance of a climate of acceptance, encouraging good social interaction, creativity, choice, personal involvement, exploration, and discovery, so the thrust and nature of this particular program may have influenced the results.

O'Donnell and Raymond (1972) reported no observable change in children's adjustment in a kindergarten conceptual-language program. Knight (1971) reported that a language experience program was not as effective in developing a favorable attitude toward reading in first grade as were two other approaches.

Finally, however, it is frequently stated that affective factors are difficult to test objectively; certain benefits of language experience programs seem to elude quantitative documentation.

Teacher Education

Before 1960, little attention was given to the language experience approach in either preservice or inservice teacher education. The lack of exposure to the language experience rationale and methodology is one factor in the reluctance of some teachers to try language experience programs. Some research has been conducted to determine the attention given to the language experience approach in teacher education programs and in school reading programs, although documentation of the actual extent of the use of the language experience approach is meager.

Hoover (1971) studied questionnaire responses of teacher educators in one hundred colleges and universities in the United States and reported that "from 1960 to 1970 professors have increased their knowledge of a language experience approach and their receptiveness to it."

Teachers may need guidance in conducting language experience programs. Both Hall (1965) and Calvert (1973) developed guides for inservice teachers to implementing a language experience program.

Carstensen (1973) reported that little emphasis was placed on encouraging pupil dictation in the activities suggested in the first-grade reading textbooks adopted for one state.

Staton (1974) reported that questionnaire responses of principals and teachers in three states indicated acceptance of the use of language experience as part of an eclectic program. M. Stauffer (1973) reported that increased achievement by pupils in a language experience program was influenced by teachers' knowledge of language experience procedures. Lane (1963), Hall (1965), and R. Stauffer (1966) reported that teachers who used the language experience approach rated it positively for practicality and effectiveness.

Language Differences

The correspondence between the language of reading material and the oral language of children is cited as a reason for using language experience approach to reading. While this correspondence is important for all children, the advantage of language experience material for those learners whose language is considered divergent or dialectically different is particularly significant. Although it is not language experience research, Levy's (1973) study seems important here. The belief that inner-city children's oral language is adequate for beginning reading instruction is supported by Levy's investigation of first-grade inner-city students' language. As a result of her analysis of vocabulary, of the mean length of T-units, and of three structures used within T-units, she concluded, "There was no evidence that the children were too deficient in linguistic abilities to learn to decode words and comprehend written communication."

Only two studies examined the dialect factor in language experience learning. Cachie (1973) compared the visual discrimination of kindergarten children who were instructed with verbatim recordings of their language and those who were instructed by a language experience method, but whose language was translated into standard English. No significant differences were found between groups. However, the two language experience programs were not compared with other methods. Cagney (1977) reported that listening comprehension of kindergarten and first-grade children was significantly better when language experience stories were presented in standard English than when language experience stories were presented in dialect. It should be noted, however, that the effects of dialect divergence in language experience programs have received very little research attention.

The existing research substantiates that linguistically different children have sufficient language background at the time of school entrance to cope with reading instruction.

Comments on Research Methodology

Since much research has concentrated generally on the comparison of the achievement of children instructed by the language experience approach with the achievement of children instructed by another method of teaching reading (usually basal readers), much of that research is subject to the flaws common to "methods" studies.

The label given to any instructional program may not adequately describe the actual program or procedures followed. Language experience research does not, in each instance, report the same type of instructional program. Research reports should include a clear description of the methods, so readers may be certain about the program that was followed. Caution should be exercised in comparing research on language experience instruction, since there is a lack of information about the actual programs followed and since there is considerable variation in the implementation of language experience techniques. The nature of skill instruction (whether a separate program or one integrated with materials created by children), the extent of the literature experiences included, and the amount of time spent, not only on reading but on related language activities in writing, speaking, and listening, should be described. In some curriculum projects, the language experience approach may be combined with other curriculum components. An eclectic approach has many advantages, but it compounds the difficulty of determining whether the features of the language experience approach contributed to pupils' achievement.

The measures used to determine reading achievement impose limitations on the conclusions to be drawn from a study. Most methods reresearch does not specifically say why or for whom a particular approach is effective. Usually, the research is reported in terms of statistical treatment of achievement scores. There is a need to go further and to examine why one method proved more effective than another method and to identify specific pupil characteristics that may be associated with success in a particular approach.

It is difficult to control the teacher variable in methods studies. The first-grade studies showed that the teacher seemed to affect achievement more than did the specific method used, and greater differences were found within methods than between methods (Bond and Dykstra 1967).

The Hawthorne effect may influence the results of methods studies. Since, in many cases, the language experience approach is new to teachers, the Hawthorne effect may weight the results in favor of this approach. On the other hand, unfamiliarity with an approach may make the teacher's job more difficult, thereby counterbalancing the Hawthorne effect.

The short time period covered in many studies is an obstacle to drawing conclusions about the long-range effects of an instructional method, though the longer the period of time studied, the greater the number of variables that cannot be controlled.

Recommendations

Since the time of the first edition of this publication in 1972, interest in the language experience approach has grown, and this can be documented in a number of ways. The number of journal articles, the amount of space in methods textbooks, the inclusion of the topic in conference programs, and the amount of doctoral research devoted to this approach have increased noticeably. Still it appears that the quantity of language experience research reported in professional journals is limited: this volume has had to rely heavily on doctoral dissertations. Though such research usually is supervised carefully, dissertations generally cannot provide longitudinal investigations nor are they often funded projects; thus, many of the language experience studies are relatively small ones. Although the language experience approach has been the focus of a number of studies, research needs remain. The recommendations for further research are organized here according to general recommendations, methodological recommendations, and recommendations related to topical areas.

General Recommendations

Additional research comparing achievement in language experience programs to achievement in other instructional programs does not appear to be needed. Since the existing body of research does substantiate that language experience is an effective way to teach reading, the trend away from methods comparison studies should be no cause for concern, even for those who want more research about the approach. The former research questions, "Which method is best?" or "Is the language experience approach effective?" are no longer appropriate ones. Instead, questions should examine the features of learning, teaching, and the learner that affect, or are affected by, elements of language experience programs. Like all research, language experience research should have a strong theoretical rationale and worthwhile research questions.

Methodological Recommendations

As is true for research in general, future language experience research should meet the standards of good research methodology. Regardless of the specific question addressed by a particular study, research in the language experience approach should include a clear description of the actual instructional program followed. Is replication possible? Using a label does not automatically mean that all programs by that name are the same. Language experience programs often vary widely. Researchers should justify their methods of evaluation in terms of appropriateness for measuring the specific variables under study. Particularly, as research seeks to report more than mere achievement, careful selection (and development) of instruments will be crucial. No study reviewed here employed criterion-referenced instruments to evaluate children's learning. The duration factor needs to be considered also. While some investigations can be quite brief, examination of certain effects of programs requires longitudinal studies.

Research Needs in Topical Areas

While there is research documentation about the effect of the language experience approach on reading achievement, reading readiness, spelling, vocabulary, writing, oral language, and affective factors, it appears that there are still research needs in these areas, as well as in others. Studies with specific research questions, instead of general investigations of achievement, should contribute considerably to the body of information about the approach. Areas of reading research are identified and some possibilities for future investigations are offered in this section.

As noted in the synthesis section of this book, additional research attention should be given to studying the use of language experience in prereading instruction. The tendency to view language experience as a beginning reading approach may have resulted in overlooking its potential as a prereading program. Future research on language experience prereading programs should be more specific than such studies have been in the past. Which factors in a child's background correlate with success, or the lack of it, in prereading language experience programs? For which specific skill areas is language experience instruction effective or ineffective? Since one advantage of language experience instruction is the excellent opportunity it provides to point out the relationship between oral and written language, this aspect should be studied. Do children who participate in a prereading program featuring language experience materials develop better concepts of reading and of word, letter, sentence, and sound than do children without such exposure? Does a language experience prereading program result in better performance on visual discrimination tasks than do commercial readiness programs? The contributions of language experience readiness programs to the tasks directly related to beginning reading probably have not been evaluated accurately by traditional readiness tests. Perhaps criterion-referenced instruments would be more appropriate for evaluating language experience instruction's contributions to performance on prereading tasks.

Although additional documentation of writing achievement fostered by language experience instruction is not needed, additional analysis of children's writing could be valuable. Although there are vocabulary and T-unit counts, explorations of other features of written expression are needed. For example, why not some development analysis of content according to organization, sequence, and other features? Why not some developmental analysis of content, to study qualities of egocentricity and externalization correlated with Piaget's stages of cognitive development?

Analyses of the spelling in language experience stories could be made to determine if there are developmental patterns in children's acquisition of knowledge of the spelling system of English. Do learners in language experience programs acquire an understanding of the nature of the spelling system more easily than do children who do not have as much opportunity to write? Detailed analyses building on Read's (1971, 1975) work could be quite informative.

Examination of the existing research in the language experience approach shows clearly that the bulk of it has been concentrated at the primary levels—especially at the first grade. There is a need for study of the language experience approach beyond the beginning reading stages.

One obvious omission is the lack of research attention to the use of the language experience approach with adult illiterates. Perhaps this can be attributed to reading educators' lack of attention to the adult illiterate in general and to tutors' reliance on very structured materials. Tutors of adults are often volunteers without background in the teaching of reading; thus, they are frequently unaware of the language experience methodology. At any rate, research exploration of the application of the language experience approach for illiterate adults appears to be much needed. Comparison of the learning-to-read processes of adult beginning readers in language experience programs with the learning-to-read processes of juvenile beginning readers is a research possibility.

Future language experience research also could explore dimensions of the reading process. Investigations of children's oral reading performance, using miscue analysis procedures, could be conducted with language experience materials: Barr (1974–1975) and Cohen (1974–1975) have reported that the instructional method used influences the types of miscues and strategies evidenced by children. However, no study investigating children's reading performance in conjunction with the language experience approach was located in this survey of the literature. What strategies are actually employed by children using the language experience approach? How do the strategies evolve or change as reading ability increases?

The nature of reading comprehension is the focus of reading researchers currently, but comprehension in terms other than those of achievement has gone unexamined in language experience studies. In a discussion of research on story comprehension, Guthrie (1977) noted that, as early as first grade, children expect stories to contain a structure. Language experience products could be analyzed according to their inclusion or omission of elements of story structure and according to possible developmental progression in children's use of those story elements. Use of story structural features could be compared with children's performance on other comprehension measures. Another question to be studied is whether children in a language experience program grasp story structure elements at the same rate or to the same degree as children instructed in other reading programs.

Ideas from the field of cognitive psychology are now being applied to reading—especially with regard to comprehension. Research is needed to investigate how children conceptualize, categorize, and organize ideas, both in producing their materials and in reading those materials. Visual imagery in reading is another topic that could be explored in conjunction with language experience materials. For example, do children who have focused on communicating with their productions use visual or mental imagery to a greater degree while reading than do children who have not used language experience materials? Examination of the cognitive styles of learners could be conducted in conjunction with language experience programs. How does a particular cognitive-style preference correlate with learning in a language experience program?

Investigations should be conducted of preservice and inservice teacher education programs to ascertain the procedures, materials, and other resources that would equip teachers to implement language experience programs. While there is some evidence that more teacher education programs give attention to this approach than prior to 1960, many teachers comment that they feel unsure about conducting language experience programs. Preparation and evaluation of language experience modules for teacher education could be a worthwhile research contribution.

Although the quantity of research on the language experience approach has increased in recent years, it appears that this increase is not nearly as great as the increase in interest in the approach. Perhaps this growing interest will result in more research analysis of the many dimensions of the language experience approach.

Bibliography

Allen, Roach Van. *Language Experiences in Communication.* Boston: Houghton Mifflin, 1976.

Allen, Roach Van. "More Ways than One." *Childhood Education* 38 (1961):108–111.

Ashton-Warner, Sylvia. *Teacher.* New York: Simon and Shuster, 1963. [ED 029 913]

Austin, Mary C., and Morrison, Coleman. *The First R: The Harvard Report on Reading in Elementary Schools.* (New York: Macmillan, 1963).

Balyeat, Ralph, and Norman, Douglas. "LEA-Cloze—Comprehension Test." *The Reading Teacher* 28 (1975):555–560.

Barnette, Eleanor A. "The Effects of a Specific Individualized Activity on the Attitudes toward Reading in the First and Second Grade." Doctoral dissertation, Arizona State University, 1970.

Barr, Rebecca. "The Effect of Instruction on Pupil Reading Strategies." *Reading Research Quarterly* 10 (1974–1975):555–582.

Baxley, Dan M. "The Utility of Forty-five Phonic Generalizations as Applied to Oral Vocabularies of Economically Limited Spanish Surname Children." Doctoral dissertation, Arizona State University, 1972.

Becker, John T. "Language Experience Approach in a Job Corps Reading Lab." *Journal of Reading* 13 (1970):281–284, 319–321.

Bennett, Stanley W. "The Key Vocabulary in Organic Reading: An Evaluation of Some of Ashton-Warner's Assumptions of Beginning Reading." Doctoral dissertation, University of Michigan, 1971.

Bond, Guy L., and Dykstra, Robert. "Interpreting the First Grade Reading Studies." In *The First Grade Reading Studies,* edited by Russell G. Stauffer, pp. 1–9. Newark, Delaware: International Reading Association, 1967. [ED 026 225]

Bond, Guy L., and Dykstra, Robert. "The Cooperative Program in First Grade Reading Instruction." *Reading Research Quarterly* 2 (1967):5–142.

Brazziel, William F., and Terrell, Mary. "For First Graders: A Good Start in School." *Elementary School Journal* 62 (1962):352–355.

Cachie, Grace. "The Effect of Two Language Experience Approaches on the Reading Comprehension, Visual Discrimination and Word Knowledge Performances of Black Kindergarten Students Who Are Speakers of Nonstandard Dialects." Doctoral dissertation, New York University, 1973.

Cagney, Margaret A. "Children's Ability to Understand Standard English and Black Dialect." *The Reading Teacher* 30 (1977): 607–610.

Calvert, John D. "An Exploratory Study to Adapt the Language Experience Approach to Remedial Seventh and Tenth Grade Mexican American Students." Doctoral dissertation, Arizona State University, 1973.

Carstensen, Leone Mabel. "Language Experiences Found in Teacher Guides for First Grade Reading Textbooks." Doctoral dissertation, University of Arizona, 1972.

Chall, Jeanne. *Learning to Read: The Great Debate.* New York: McGraw Hill, 1967.

Christensen, Katharine E. "Effects upon Children's Oral Syntactic Language Development under Two Kindergarten Programs." Doctoral dissertation, University of Delaware, 1971.

———. "Language Facility of Kindergarten Children." *Elementary English* 49 (1972):1107–1111, 1119.

Cohen, Alice Sheff. "Oral Reading Errors of First Grade Children Taught by a Code Emphasis Approach." *Reading Research Quarterly* 10 (1974–1975):616–650.

Cohen, S. Alan, and Kornfield, Gita S. "Oral Vocabulary and Beginning Reading in Disadvantaged Children." *The Reading Teacher* 24 (1970):33–38.

Cox, Vivian E. "Reciprocal Oracy/Literacy Recognition Skills in the Language Production of Language Experience Students." Doctoral dissertation, University of Arizona, 1971.

Cramer, Ronald L. "An Investigation of the Spelling Achievement of Two Groups of First-Grade Classes on Phonologically Regular and Irregular Words and in Written Composition." Doctoral dissertation, University of Delaware, 1968.

———. "An Investigation of First-Grade Spelling Achievement." *Elementary English* 47 (1970):230–237.

Duquette, Raymond J. "An Experimental Study Comparing the Effect of a Specific Program of Sight Vocabulary upon Reading and Writing Achievement of Selected First and Second Grade Children." Doctoral dissertation, Arizona State University, 1970.

Dykstra, Robert. "Summary of the Second-Grade Phase of the Cooperative Research Program in Primary Reading Instruction." *Reading Research Quarterly* 4 (1968):49–70.

Dzama, Mary Ann. "A Comparative Study of Natural vs. Frequency Control Sight Vocabularies on the Basis of Forty-five Phonic Generalizations." Doctoral dissertation, University of Virginia, 1972.

———. "Comparing Use of Generalizations of Phonics in LEA, Basal Vocabulary." *The Reading Teacher* 28 (1975):466–472.

National Right to Read Effort. *Effective Reading Programs.* Urbana, Illinois: ERIC Clearinghouse on Reading and Communication Skills, 1975.

Gardner, D. E. M. *Testing Results in the Infant School.* London: Methuen & Company, 1942.

Giles, Douglas E. "The Effect of Two Approaches to Reading Instruction upon the Oral Language Development of First Grade Pupils." Doctoral dissertation, North Texas State University, 1966.

Guthrie, John. "Research Views—Story Comprehension." *The Reading Teacher* 30 (1977):574—577.

Hahn, Harry T. "Three Approaches to Beginning Reading Instruction—ITA, Language Experience and Basic Readers." *The Reading Teacher* 19 (1966):590—594.

——. "Three Approaches to Beginning Reading Instruction, ITA, Language Experience and Basic Readers—Extended into Second Grade." *The Reading Teacher* 20 (1967):711—715.

——. *Teaching Reading and Language Skills in Grades Two and Three.* Rochester, Michigan: Oakland University, 1968. [ED 022 645]

Hall, MaryAnne. "The Development and Evaluation of a Language Experience Approach to Reading with First-Grade Culturally Disadvantaged Children." Doctoral dissertation, University of Maryland, 1965.

——. *Teaching Reading as a Language Experience.* Columbus: Charles E. Merrill, 1976.

Harris, Albert J. "The Effective Teacher of Reading." *The Reading Teacher* 23 (1969):195—204, 238.

Harris, Albert J., and Morrison, Coleman. "The CRAFT Project: A Final Report." *The Reading Teacher* 22 (1969):335—340.

Harris, Albert J., and Serwer, Blanche L. "Comparing Reading Approaches in First Grade Teaching with Disadvantaged Children." *The Reading Teacher* 19 (1966):631—635.

Harris, Albert J.; Serwer, Blanche L.; and Gold, Lawrence. "Comparing Reading Approaches in First Grade Teaching with Disadvantaged Children—Extended into Second Grade." *The Reading Teacher* 20 (1967):698—703.

Harris, Gary R. "The Effects of Communication Skills through Authorship: A Language Experience Supplement on the Development of Reading Skills with Primary Students." Doctoral dissertation, University of Idaho, 1972.

Henderson, Edmund H.; Estes, Thomas H.; and Stonecash, Susan. "An Exploratory Study of Word Acquisition among First-Graders at Midyear in a Language Experience Approach." *Journal of Reading Behavior* 4 (1972):21—31.

Hildreth, Gertrude. "Experience Related Reading for School Beginners." *Elementary English* 42 (1965):280—297.

Hoover, Irene. "Historical and Theoretical Development of a Language Experience Approach to Teaching Reading in Selected Teacher Education Institutions." Doctoral dissertation, University of Arizona, 1971.

Horn, Thomas D. "Three Methods of Developing Reading Readiness in Spanish Speaking Children in First Grade." *The Reading Teacher* 20 (1966): 38—42.

Kelly, Ann Marie. "Sight Vocabularies and Experience Stores." *Elementary English* 52 (1977):327—328.

Kendrick, William M. "A Comparative Study of Two First Grade Language Arts Programs." *The Reading Teacher* 20 (1966):25—30.

Kendrick, William M., and Bennett, Clayton L. "A Comparative Study of Two First Grade Language Arts Programs—Extended into Second Grade." *The Reading Teacher* 20 (1967):747—755.

Kingston, Albert J., and Weaver, Wendell W. "Feasibility of Cloze Techniques for Teaching and Evaluating Culturally Disadvantaged Beginning Readers." *The Journal of Social Psychology* (December 1970):205—214.

Lamb, Pose. "The Language Experience Approach to Teaching Beginning Reading to Culturally Disadvantaged Pupils." Final Report Project No. 0-E-005, Grant No. OEG-5-70-0013 (010). Washington, D.C.: U. S. Department of Health, Education and Welfare, Office of Education, Bureau of Research, 1971. [ED 059 314]

Lane, Kenneth Boyd. "A Description, Analysis and Evaluation of Three Approaches to the Teaching of Reading." Doctoral dissertation, North Texas State University, 1963.

Lee, Dorris M., and Allen, R. V. *Learning to Read through Experience.* 2nd ed. New York: Appleton-Century-Crofts, 1963. [ED 027 067]

Levy, Beatrice K. "Is the Oral Language of Inner City Children Adequate for Beginning Reading Instruction?" *Research in the Teaching of English* 7 (1973):51—60.

Madison, John P. "NCTE/ERIC Report: The Language Experience Approach to Teaching Reading." *Elementary English* 48 (1971): 682—689.

Mallett, W. Graham. "A Comparative Study of the Language Experience Approach with Junior High Native Indian Students." Doctoral dissertation, Arizona State University, 1975.

McCanne, Roy. "Approaches to First Grade English Reading Instruction for Children from Spanish Speaking Homes." *The Reading Teacher* 19 (1966):70–75.

McC. Gallager, Jo Anne. "Vocabulary Retention of Lower-Class Students in Language Experience and in Basal Approaches to the Teaching of Reading." Doctoral dissertation, University of South Carolina, 1975.

Mendenhall, Betty J. "Developing Self-Acceptance and Reading Achievement among Second Grade Chicano Children." Doctoral dissertation, University of Colorado, 1973.

Meriam, Junius L. "Avoiding Difficulties in Learning to Read." *Educational Method* 9 (1930):413–419.

———. "An Activity Curriculum in a School of Mexican Children." *Journal of Experimental Education* 1 (1933):304–308.

O'Donnell, C. Michael, and Raymond, Dorothy. "Developing Reading Readiness in the Kindergarten." *Elementary English* 49 (1972); 768–771.

Oehlkers, William J. "The Contribution of Creative Writing to Reading Achievement in the Language Experience Approach." Doctoral dissertation, University of Delaware, 1971.

Owens, Francis Louis. "A Study of Creative Writing Ability of Third Grade Students in a Communication Skills through Authorship Program." Doctoral dissertation, University of Idaho, 1972.

Packer, Athol. "Ashton-Warner's Key Vocabulary for the Disadvantaged." *The Reading Teacher* 23 (1970):559–564.

Read, Charles. "Pre-School Children's Knowledge of English Phonology." *Harvard Educational Review* 41 (1971):1–34.

———. *Children's Categorization of Speech Sounds in English.* Research Report, No. 17. Urbana, Illinois: National Council of Teachers of English, 1975. [ED 112 426]

Reindeau, Betty A. "An Exploratory Investigation of the Effect of Two Differing Approaches of Reading Instruction on the Self-Social Concepts of First-Grade Children." Doctoral dissertation, American Univeristy, 1973.

San Diego Department of Education. *Improving Reading Instruction: Description of Three Approaches to the Teaching of Reading.* Monograph 2 (1961).

Schomer, Joseph H. "A Study of the Reading Achievement of First and Second Grade Students in a Communication Skills through

Authorship Program." Doctoral dissertation, University of Idaho, 1971.

Serwer, Blanche L. "Linguistic Support for a Method of Teaching Beginning Reading to Black Children." *Reading Research Quarterly* 4 (1969):449—467.

Staton, Janette. "Initial Reading Practices in Open Education Environments in the Midprarie States." Doctoral dissertation, Oklahoma State University, 1974.

Stauffer, Marian A. "Comparative Effects of a Language Arts Approach and Basal Reader Approach to First Grade Reading Achievement." Doctoral dissertation, University of Delaware, 1973.

Stauffer, Russell G. "The Effectiveness of Language Arts and Basic Reading Approaches to First Grade Reading Instruction." *The Reading Teacher* 20 (1966):18—24.

———. *The Language-Experience Approach to the Teaching of Reading.* New York: Harper and Row, 1970. [ED 040 025]

———. *Action Research in L.E.A. Instructional Procedures.* Newark, Delaware: University of Delaware, 1976.

Stauffer, Russell G., and Cramer, Ronald L. "Reading Specialists in an Occupational Training Program." *The Reading Teacher* 20 (1967):525—531.

Stauffer, Russell G., and Hammond, W. Dorsey. "The Effectiveness of Language Arts and Basic Reader Approaches to First Grade Reading Instruction—Extended into Second Grade." *The Reading Teacher* 20 (1967):740—746.

Stauffer, Russell G., and Hammond, W. Dorsey. "The Effectiveness of Language Arts and Basic Reader Approaches to First Grade Reading Instruction—Extended to the Third Grade." *Reading Research Quarterly* 4 (1969):468—499.

Stauffer, Russell G.; Hammond, W. Dorsey; Oehlkers, William; and Houseman, Ann. *Effectiveness of a Language Arts and Basal Reader Approach to First Grade Reading—Extended into Sixth Grade.* Newark, Delaware: University of Delaware, 1972.

Stauffer, Russell G., and Pikulski, John J. "A Comparison and Measure of Oral Language Growth," *Elementary English* 51 (1974):1151—1155.

Stockler, Dolores S. "Responses to the Language Experience Approach by Black, Culturally Different, Inner-City Students Experiencing Reading Disability in Grades Five and Eleven." Doctoral dissertation, Indiana University, 1971.

Vilscek, Elaine C. "What Research Has Shown about the Language-Experience Program." In *A Decade of Innovations: Approaches to Beginning Reading*, pp. 9–25. Newark, Delaware: International Reading Association, 1968. [ED 075 810]

Vilscek, Elaine, and Cleland, Donald L. *Two Approaches to Reading Instruction: Final Report*. Pittsburgh: University of Pittsburgh, 1968. [ED 022 647]

Vilscek, Elaine D.; Cleland, Donald L.; and Bilka, Loisanne. "Coordinating and Integrating Language Arts Instruction." *The Reading Teacher* 21 (1967):3–10.

Vilscek, Elaine; Morgan, Lorraine; and Cleland, Donald L. "Coordinating and Integrating Language Arts Instruction in First Grade." *The Reading Teacher* 20 (1966):31–37.

Weber, Elaine M. "An Investigation of the Effects of Two Reading Readiness Programs Which Were Administered by Parents to Their Post-Kindergarten Children on Measures of Readiness, Listening and Beginning Reading." Doctoral dissertation, Michigan State University, 1975.

Wells, Timothy M. "An Investigation Designed to Test the Feasibility of Using Visual Literacy Techniques and the Language Experience Approach to Reading to Develop the Reading Abilities of Remedial Fourth Grade Readers." Doctoral dissertation, Michigan State University, 1975.

Willardson, Marlyn L. "A Study of the Writing Ability of Second Grade Students in a Communication Skills through Authorship Program." Doctoral dissertation, University of Idaho, 1971.

Wilson, Robert M., and Parkey, Nancy. "A Modified Reading Program in a Middle School," *Journal of Reading* 13 (1970):447–552.

Wrightstone, J. Wayne. "Evaluation of the Experiment with the Activity Program in the New York City Elementary Schools." *Journal of Educational Research* 38 (1944):252–257.

Wrightstone, J. Wayne. "Research Related to Experience Records and Basal Readers," *The Reading Teacher* 5 (1951):5–6.

Richard Lee (Booksellers) P/L
55 Cardigan Street
Carlton, 3053
Book Importers & Distributors